D1284347

For my nieces and nephew:

Zachary, Arianna, Alexa, Autumn
&
Ava

Written & Created by: Jason Van Woeart
Illustrated by: Beth Scuotto

The Adventures of Marina Cat: Who ate my food? - 1st ed.
ISBN: 978-1-7360045-0-0

The adventures of
Marina Cat
who ate my food?

Written & Created by: Jason Van Woeart
Illustrated by: Beth Ann Scuotto

It was yet another peaceful
and sunny day at the waterfront
for Marina Cat.

The birds were chirping above in deep conversation as townies fished off the pier. The sound of laughter and excitement came from the cold water as jet skis zoomed by.

As the town clock slowly ticked towards 6:00p.m, Marina Cat's belly began to rumble from hunger. She patiently watched the clock as she waited for her human friends to deliver her dinner.

Night time arrived and the waterfront was quiet. With the exception of frogs, crickets, and the ocean waves gently rocking anchored boats.

Marina Cat had one more bite of food
before heading off to sleep.

With a belly full of food,
Marina Cat fell asleep for the night.

Morning came and Marina Cat yawned, stretched, and made her way to her food bowl for breakfast. It wasn't until she got to her bowl that she found her food was gone!

Someone or something had eaten all of
Marina Cat's food.
"The food must have been eaten while I
was asleep!"
She thought to herself.

"I know! Tonight I will stay up past my bedtime and see if they come back." Marina Cat decided to herself.

Another peaceful and sunny day went by at the water front. Marina Cat's human friends delivered her dinner and shortly after she eagerly waited for night to fall.

Marina Cat was determined to stay up past her bedtime and catch the culprit who ate her food. As time slowly went by she began to drift off into a deep sleep.

Morning came and Marina Cat
woke. Realizing she fell asleep,
Marina Cat frantically ran to
her food bowl to find it ....

"If only I had not eaten so much food last night I could have stayed up late!", Marina said regretfully. "I know! If I nap today I wont be as tired tonight. Then I will catch the culprit who has been eating my food!"

Marina quietly poked her head out of the bushes to find, "A baby chipmunk! How adorable!" Marina thought to herself.
"Hello there!" Marina cheerfully greeted the chipmunk.

As Marina Cat made her way out of the bushes to introduce herself to the chipmunk she was suprised to find....

A crowd of animals of different shapes, colors, and sizes. The animals were in a single-file line behind the chipmunk as they all waited for their turn to eat her food!

"Are you all new in town?" Marina asked. The chipmunk replied, "We all moved here two nights ago from Central Park. We haven't been able to find food since we got off the ferry boat from NYC. I'm sorry we are eating your food without asking."

"You would do that for us?," asked the Fox. "Of course!" said Marina Cat. "It will be nice to have new furry-faced friends here at the waterfront!"

"My name is Marina Cat and I have lived here for several years. Welcome to the water front! Tomorrow morning I will give everyone the grand tour! Until then, good night everyone! and welcome!"

With a full heart, Marina Cat finally laid down to sleep and slowly drifted off to dreamland. Marina couldn't help but smile knowing she did the right thing by sharing her food, and welcoming new friends even though they looked and sounded different.

About the Author

Jason Van Woeart was inspired to write this book by a very friendly & clean stray cat at his local marina that he has been feeding for the past few years. During his visits to see Marina, he has witnessed numerous types of wild life snacking on Marina's food and came up with the idea for this book.

Jason's house cats, Astin & Martin were both adopted from The Northshore Animal League America, hence the decision to donate 25% of proceeds to their organization for the amazing care and love they show to animals in need.

Jason works full-time, is a full-time education student at Kean University, and lives in Carteret, NJ.

*The North Shore Animal League America has no affiliation, participation, or partnership and does not endorse this book or it's author.

Thank You:

Van Woeart and Parisio family for always accepting and supporting me. Especially Mom, Dad, Jeff, and Janai.

Jason Pablo for your encouragement, for always feeding Marina when I don't have time because of school, and for being the animal advocate that you are.
I love you!

Beth Scuotto for your impressive artistic talent and for always cheering me on no matter what I do in life. This book would not have been made possible if it wasn't for you.
I will forever be grateful.

24639770R00018